MoonCave Crystals

Gemstone Healing Guide
A Healing Apothecary

Table of Contents

Acknowledgements 3

Credits 3

Prologue 4

Physical Healing 5

Emotional Healing 29

Higher Self 43

The Chakras 57

Crystal Information 63

Store Bound Rock Hound .64

Cleaning Crystals 67

Thoughts on Crystal Storage 71

Elixir Warnings 73

**References, Resources and Recommended
Reading** 75

Y0-DBV-706

First Edition – January 2005.

ISBN: 0-9703278-7-1.

Printed in the United States of America.

Gemstone Healing Guide is published by Technicraft Design, PO Box 33472, Seattle, WA 98133-3472. 1-800-567-1334. http://www.technicraft.com

For more crystal information, see: http://www.mooncavecrystals.com or call MoonCave Crystals at 1-360-432-2340.

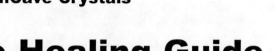
Gemstone Healing Guide
A Healing Apothecary

Credits

Written by:	Layout and Design:
Kristi Huggins	Justin Dagna
Edited by:	**Cover Art by**
Justin Dagna Kristi Huggins	Jan Custers

Acknowledgements

I would like to express my sincere gratitude to those who have made this labor of love so easy and joyous for me:

- To Justin and Sally Dagna, for their unending patience, knowledge, support and hard work, not only on this book but on a score of other projects as well.
- To Linda Glendenning and Elson Baugh whose total acceptance and crystal "know how" set me on this path some years ago.
- To Te Rangitahi Pumau whose support and love throughout this process helped me to believe in myself and the importance of what I had to say.
- To the "MoonCave family" of clients and customers who teach me something new every day and remind me that it is not about "clients" and "customers" but about family and love. You are ALL my family and I love you dearly.

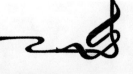

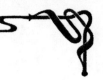

Prologue

We each carry with us a special gift--that of intuition. We might choose a crystal or stone because "it's sparkly!" or just a sense of "Ohhhhh, pretty!". We may choose because we are drawn to a certain color or shape.

This is intuition at its finest!

While there are many books at our disposal to read and learn about crystals, I feel that these are secondary to our own intuition, which guides us, always, in the right direction. Some prefer to read about many crystals and their properties and make a list based on what the books say. I feel that one should always look, touch, or intuitively "feel" the crystal that one is drawn to FIRST--then used the book as a secondary tool, afterwards. Trust yourself above all else.

This compilation is a comprehensive guide only. It is divided into three sections: physical healing, emotional healing and higher self. You will not find any crystals/minerals/gemstones listed here that are rare or difficult to find.

Disclaimer:

The information contained in this Healing Stone Apothecary is not meant to replace diagnosis and treatment by a qualified medical practitioner. All recommendations herein contained are derived from research, informational handouts, books and intuition. No expressed or implied guarantee as to the effects of their uses can be given nor liability taken.

Research was done using a number of books and guides which can be viewed in the Resources and Credits section located in the back of this guide.

Physical Healing

Long Distance Healing

Jeffrey's Quartz
Danburite, Pink
Goldstone, Blue
Labradorite

Abundance

Aventurine, Green
Citrine
Fuchsite
Malachite
Moonstone
Moss Agate
Ruby
Topaz

Abdominal

Blue Lace Agate – colic
Chrysotile – reduces toxins
Garnet – relieves pressure
Variscite – abdominal distention
Wulfenite – energizing to area

Abrasions

Conichalcite
Dioptase
Euclase
Halite
Jadeite (lilac-colored jade)
Tourmaline

Aches (General)

Aragonite
Blue Lace Agate
Brazilian Agate
Charoite
Dendritic Agate
Euclase
Lodestone

Acne

Amethyst (in elixir)

Addictions

Amethyst – alcohol addiction
Barite – assisting in recovery
Blue Calcite – pharmaceutical
    detoxification
Iolite – alcohol addiction
Kunzite – helps to overcome
Labradorite
Lazulite
Phenacite – helps to overcome
Zeolites (Okenite, Apophyllite,
    Prehnite, Chabazite, Natrolite)

ADHD

Lepidolite
Rutilated Quartz

AIDS / HIV

Amethyst
Carnelian
Clear Quartz
Conichalcite
Dioptase – for increase in T-cell
    count
Euclase
Jadeite
Lapis Lazuli
Sugilite
Tourmaline

Allergies

Carnelian – pollen allergies
Ellensburg Blue Agate
Smithsonite
Zircon

Altitude Sickness

Jet
Sapphire

Alzheimer's

Chalcedony, Blue/Purple
Buddstone – general
Galena – confusion

Anemia

Bloodstone
Copper
Hedenbergite
Hematite
Red Garnet
Kunzite
Ruby
Tiger's Eye
Tourmaline

Anger

Alabaster – diminishing internal
    anger
Amethyst – dissolves anger
Bloodstone – dissolves anger
Blue Lace Agate
Carnelian – protects against
    fear/rage
Chrysocolla – reduces anger
Howlite – eliminates stress and
rage
Manganocalcite
Peridot
Rose Quartz
Smithsonite
Stilbite
Wavellite

Anxiety

Amethyst
Aventurine
Green Millennium Stone
Hemimorphite – anxiety in chil-
    dren
Howlite
Lapis Lazuli
Lepidolite
Lithium in Quartz
Manganocalcite
Smithsonite
Black Tourmaline

Anorexia

Garnet (Grossular/Massive Pink)
Rose Quartz

Arthritis

Amber – bursitis, general
Blue Lace Agate – bursitis
Boji Stones
Charoite
Chrysocolla
Copper
Diopside
Emerald
Fluorite
Garnet
Malachite – bursitis

Moonstone
Pyrite
Rhodonite
Scapolite
Tourmaline, Black

Asthma

Amber
Azurite
Blue Lace Agate
Carnelian
Coral
Lapis Lazuli
Larimar
Malachite
Morganite
Tiger's Eye

Autism

Moldavite
Sugilite

Back

Carnelian – injuries & tension
    reliever
Hematite – aches
Lapis Lazuli – pain
Magnetite – aches
Vanadinite – backbone in general

Bacterial & Viral Infections

Calcite, Green – rids body of
    infection
Chalcopyrite – reduces fever and
    inflammation
Copper – fights infection, cleans-

es wound
Fluorite – for colds, flu, and
    staph. and strep. infections
Jet – colds
Malachite
Moss Agate – relieves symptoms
Sulfur

Balance-Physical Body

Double Terminated Quartz
Ametrine
Carnelian
Chiastolite (Andaluscite)
Copper
Fire Agate
Snowflake Obsidian
Zebra Stone

Birthing

Calcite, Orange – assists in
    birthing
Lapis Lazuli – help in birthing
    process
Malachite – easing of birthing
    process
Moonstone – promotes ease in
    pregnancy
Onyx, Black
Opal
Peridot – facilitator of birthing
    process

Bleeding, Stop

Bloodstone
Ruby

Blood

Amethyst – cleanser, used for clots

Azurite – strengthens blood in general

Bloodstone – circulation, cleanser

Carnelian – oxygenates

Copper – increases flow, cleanser

Eudialyte – purifies blood, circulation

Garnet – Cleanser

Lodestone

Manganocalcite – clotting

Marcasite – blood stream cleanser

Moss Agate – Circulation

Orbicular Sea Jasper – increases flow

Ruby – blood cleanser

Sodalite – purifies blood, cleansing

Staurolite – purifies blood

Blood Pressure

Aventurine, Red – pressure equalizer

Tourmaline – to equalize blood pressure

Charoite – to equalize and regulate blood pressure

Cacoxenite – for low blood pressure

Calcite, Red – for low blood pressure

Ruby – for low blood pressure

Sodalite – for low blood pressure

Tourmaline – for low blood pressure

Chrysoprase – for high blood pressure

Dioptase – for high blood pressure

Emerald – for high blood pressure

Scapolite – for high blood pressure

Tourmaline, Black or Green – general

Body

Amber – detoxifies, draws disease out

Botswana Agate – oxygenates body

Celestite – draws disease from tissues

Dolomite – cleanses, energizes

Magnesite – odor

Malachite – cleanses, detoxifies

Peridot – physical body, general

Quantum Quattro Silica – all purpose

Sodalite – cleanses

Smoky Quartz – cleanses

Thulite – cleanses

Vesuvianite – physical body, general

Zoisite – energizer, physical vitality

Bones

Amber – bone marrow healing

Apatite – for bone problems or illness

Axinite – mends breaks and fractures

Barite Rose – general healing, aching

Calcite – general healing, bone health
Copper – general healing
Dolomite
Fluorite – strengthens bone, tissue
Fluorite, Purple – bone marrow
Gypsum – strengthens
Howlite – strengthens
Lapis Lazuli – strengthens skeletal structure
Magnetite – for bone aching
Malachite – for bone aching
Onyx – bone marrow healing
Scapolite – for bone problems or illness
Selenite – strengthens, for bone illness
Zoisite – general

Brain

Amber – strengthens brain tissues
Amethyst – brain relaxation
Aventurine – general
Azurite – general
Blue Lace Agate – balances fluid
Calcite – energizes
Hemimorphite – for brain injuries
Indicolite – general
Kunzite – general
Labradorite – stimulates mental activity
Lapis Lazuli – improves function
Nuummit – stimulates mental acuity
Pyrite – general
Ruby – general
Sapphire – general
Sodalite – general

Stilbite – treatment of disorders
Thulite – brain damage
Tourmaline, Green – general
Zircon – brain damage

Bruises

Blue Lace Agate
Hematite, in conjunction w/Rose Quartz

Bulimia

Garnet (Grossular, Massive Pink)
Orthoclase
Rose Quartz
Stibnite

Burns

Agate
Chrysoprase
Lazulite
Quartz, Clear
Rose Quartz – relieves blistering

Cancer

Amethyst – general
Aventurine, Red – healing
Bloodstone – general
Covellite – general
Dioptase – general
Emerald – Skin
Garnet, Green – general
Jade – general
Larimar – general
Malachite – general
Rhodonite – healing
Smoky Quartz – general
Sugilite – healing

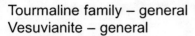
Tourmaline family – general
Vesuvianite – general

Chemotherapy

Herkimer Diamond
Smoky Quartz

Chronic Fatigue

Iolite
Serpentine
Zincite

Chronic Pain Relief

Jade (Blue)

Circulation

Bloodstone – blood circulation
Cacoxenite – general
Citrine – blood circulation
Copper – increases blood flow
Eudialyte – blood circulation
Fire Agate – blood circulation
Galena – blood circulation
Garnet – blood circulation
Jasper, Red – improves &
    strengthens
Moonstone – treatment of disor-
    der
Moss Agate – blood/lymph circu-
    lation
Nephrite – blood/lymphatic circu-
    lation
Tektite – blood circulation
Thulite – blood circulation
Tiger Eye, Blue (Hawkeye)

Colds

Amber
Blue Lace Agate
Carnelian
Coral
Emerald
Fluorite, Rainbow
Jet
Larimar
Moss Agate
Sulfur

Colon

Bloodstone – general
Calcite, Blue – cleansing
Carnelian – general
Garnet – cleansing
Scapolite – general

Coma

Lapis Lazuli
Moldavite Tektite
Tanzanite

Concentration

Apatite
Fluorite
Hematite
Onyx
Pearl
Topaz
Tourmaline

Congestion

Azurite/Malachite Combination

Constipation

Amber
Calcite (Blue)
Orange Millennium Stone
Ruby

Coughs

Amber
Aquamarine
Topaz

Cramps

Bloodstone
Iolite

Crohn's Disease

Diopside

Deafness

Hemimorphite
Onyx
Rhodonite
Tourmaline

Dehydration

Jasper, Bracciated Red
Mookaite Agate
Moss Agate
Mica
Stilbite

Dementia

Buddstone
Rutilated Quartz

Dental Pain/Problems

Blue Lace Agate
Fluorite

Depression

Amber
Amethyst – stabilizes mental dis-
    orders
Aragonite
Botswana Agate, Pink
Kyanite, Green – reduces
Lapis Lazuli – reduces
Lepidolite – reduces
    stress/depression
Lithium – manic depression
Peridot
Petalite – reduces
Rose Quartz
Septurian Nodule
Staurolite – depression, addictive
    traits
Tourmaline, Green – reduces
Vesuvianite

Detoxifying the Body

Amber – etheric
Amegreen – cleanses/detoxifies
Amethyst – general, mental &
    spiritual
Bloodstone – general
Carnelian
Copper – general
Charoite
Chlorite included in Quartz
Emerald
Jade
Lapis Lazuli – etheric and spiritu-
    al

Malachite
Peridot
Topaz – general

Diabetes

Citrine
Datolite
Jade
Serpentine
Sulfur
Zincite

Digestion

Citrine – improve
Dolomite – improve
Garnet (Grossularite, yellow) – cleanse
Moss Agate – improve
Sunstone – improve

DNA Damage

Pyrite
Quantum Quattro Silica
Variscite

Dyslexia

Hemimorphite
Sugilite

Ears (Hearing)

Amazonite – ear ache
Amethyst – treatment of hearing disorders
Amber – ear ache
Calcite, Orange
Celestite – increases range of hearing
Hiddenite
Lapis Lazuli – cellular restructuring
Rhodonite – hearing loss
Sapphire
Snowflake Obsidian
Tourmaline – hearing loss

Eczema

Sapphire

Edema (Water/Fluid Retention)

Aqua Aura
Aquamarine
Carnelian
Jade
Moonstone

Emphysema

Amber
Amethyst
Aqua Aura
Dioptase
Emerald
Larimar
Malachite
Morganite
Rose Quartz
Tiger Eye

Epilepsy

Jasper
Jet
Lapis Lazuli
Mesolite

Onyx
Pearl
Selenite
Sugilite
Tourmaline

Exhaustion

Cacoxenite
Calcite, Honey
Garnet

Eyes

Apophyllite – improving vision
Aqua Aura – watering of the eyes
Aquamarine – watering of the eyes
Bloodstone – failing eyesight
Blue Lace Agate – eye infections
Chrysoprase – inflammation
Citrine – increases visual abilities
Fire Agate – general eye disorders
Fluorite, Blue – treatment of
Emerald – eye strain, tired eyes
Jade – eye disease
Labradorite – clarify the eyes
Lapis Lazuli – general eye problems
Mica – brings sparkle to the eyes
Nuummit – general
Opal – clarifies and strengthens
Pearl – general
Peridot – astigmatism and near-sightedness
Rosasite – general
Sapphire – eye infection
Scapolite – cataracts
Tiger Eye – night vision
Tourmaline, Green – general

Turquoise – cataracts
Ulexite – strengthens eye muscles

Fainting

Lapis Lazuli

Fatigue

Apophyllite
Dendritic Agate
Garnet, Red
Iolite
Rose Quartz
Rutilated Quartz
Tiger Iron

Feet

Apophyllite
Heulendite
Onyx – burning
Smoky Quartz
Sunstone – aching feet

Fertility

Astrophyllite – reproductive disorders
Carnelian – improve fertility
Chrysoprase – stimulate fertility
Cinnabar – correcting deficiencies
Danburite – general
Gypsum – stimulates fertility
Jade – general
Moonstone – enhances fertility
Rose Quartz – stimulates fertility
Rubellite – treats disorder of system

Tiger Eye – treats disorder of system

Unakite – stimulates healthy pregnancy

Zoisite – general

Fever

Chiastolite
Coral
Emerald
Jet
Opal
Quartz
Ruby

Fractures

Calcite
Fluorite
Magnetite
Onyx

Gallbladder

Calcite
Carnelian
Citrine
Danburite
Dolomite
Fluorite
Hiddenite
Tiger's Eye

Glands

Aquamarine – swollen glands
Blue Lace Agate – swollen glands
Cacoxenite – stimulates glands
Mother of Pearl – glandular fever
Nephrite – therapeutic

Sodalite – therapeutic
Topaz – swollen glands
Uvite – therapeutic

Gout

Charoite
Topaz
Tourmaline

Headaches

Amber – to relieve headaches
Amethyst – to relieve headaches
Blue Lace Agate
Charoite – general
Citrine – general
Dioptase – migraines
Fluorite, Blue
Hematite– to relieve headaches
Jet – migraines
Lapis Lazuli – to prevent headaches
Larimar – sinus headaches
Moonstone – general
Nuummit – relieves discomfort
Sugilite – excellent reliever of pain
Turquoise – to relieve headaches

Health

Aventurine – promotes health
Magnetite – attracts health

Heart

Abalone – strengthens
Amber – strengthens
Amazonite – strengthens
Aqua Aura – strengthens

Aventurine, Green – treatment of
Cacoxenite
Chrysoprase – treats disorders of
    heart
Dioptase– prevention
Dolomite – relieves pain of heart
    attack
Emerald – disorders of the heart
Garnet, Red – heart and blood
Hematite – inflammation
Manganocalcite
Rhodonite – heart disorders
Strawberry Quartz
Tourmaline, Black – heart disease
Tourmaline, Green – regenerates
    heart
Zoisite – improves heart disor-
    ders

Heartburn

Carnelian – to prevent
Dioptase – to relieve
Dolomite – to relieve
Peridot – to relieve
Quartz, Clear – eases, relieves

Herpes

Conichalcite
Dolomite
Eudialyte
Jadeite
Lapis Lazuli

Hip Pain

Azurite
Petrified Wood

Hyperactivity

Cerussite
Garnet
Hemimorphite
Ulexite

Hypoglycemia

Chrysoprase, Dendritic

Hypothermia

Zincite

Hypothyroidism

Iolite

Immune System

Amethyst – strengthens
Aragonite – strengthens
Emerald – strengthens
Eudialyte – strengthens
Green Millennium Stone
    (Quartzite)
Jade
Lapis Lazuli – strengthens
Lazulite – strengthens
Malachite – strengthens
Quartz, Clear – strengthens
Quantum Quattro Silica
Rosasite – strengthens
Shaman Stones
Smithsonite
Tourmaline – Strengthens

Impotency

Amazonite

Variscite

Indigestion

Blue Lace Agate
Jasper
Peridot
Tourmaline

Infection

Blue Lace Agate – to relieve
Calcite, Green – Bacterial/Viral
Carnelian – Bacterial/Viral
Chalcopyrite – Bacterial/Viral
Copper – Bacterial/Viral, poultice
   use
Galena
Malachite – to prevent
Opal – Bacterial/Viral
Selenite
Sulfur

Infertility

Carnelian
Chrysoprase
Gypsum
Jade
Malachite
Moonstone
Rose Quartz
Rubellite
Smoky Quartz
Tiger Eye
Unakite

Insomnia

Amethyst
Chrysoprase

Hematite
Jade
Lapis Lazuli
Lepidolite
Mica
Moonstone
Selenite
Sodalite
Zoisite

Intestines

Amber
Carnelian
Fluorite, Green
Garnet
Jasper
Peridot
Psilomelane
Ruby
Scapolite

Irritability

Pearl
Manganocalcite
Serpentine

Itching

Azurite
Dolomite
Malachite

Jaundice

Jadeite

Joints

Aragonite – to strengthen

Azurite – for disability of
Calcite – general
Hematite – inflammation
Magnetite – general
Rhodonite – general

Kidneys

Amber
Bloodstone
Cacoxenite – aids
Calcite, Honey – stimulates
Carnelian
Charoite – aids
Citrine
Clear Quartz
Fluorite – aids
Garnet – aids
Nephrite
Nuummit
Ruby in Zoisite
Scapolite – aids
Septurian Nodule – aids
Sunstone – aids

Labor Pains

Lapis Lazuli
Tiger Iron

Laryngitis

Amber
Blue Lace Agate
Lapis Lazuli
Sodalite
Tourmaline, Blue (Indicolite)
Zincite, Blue/Grey

Legs

Azurite – strengthens knees
Aquamarine – to strengthen
Garnet – to strengthen
Hematite – for cramping
Jasper – to strengthen
Ruby – to strengthen
Smoky Quartz – to strengthen

Liver

Aquamarine – general
Azurite/Malachite – general
Bloodstone – purifies
Calcite, Blue – cleanses
Carnelian – general
Charoite – improves degraded
    condition
Danburite – liver ailments
Emerald – aids function
Fluorite, Yellow
Garnet – general
Jade
Lazulite – cleanses
Manganocalcite – aids function
Peridot – general
Sodalite – cleanses
Sphalerite – general
Stilbite – cleanses
Sunstone – cleanses
Zircon – general

Lungs

Amber – for lack of breath
Amazonite – general lung condi-
    tions
Ammonite – treatment of disor-
    ders
Bloodstone – Lung congestion

Calcite, Green – general
Chrysocolla – aids in lung conditions
Dioptase
Dolomite – oxygenation
Kunzite
Malachite – strengthens
Morganite – treatment of disease, clears
Peridot – general
Pyrite – general
Rhodochrosite
Rhodonite – treatment of emphysema
Rose Quartz – general
Rutilated Quartz – bronchitis
Serpentine – strengthens
Tiger's Eye

Lymphatic System

Amber – Lymph problems
Larimar – Lymph problems
Sodalite – general
Sulfur – general
Tourmaline – general
Zincite – general

Memory

Carnelian
Clear Quartz
Emerald
Fluorite
Moss Agate
Pyrite
Rhodochrosite
Rhodonite

Menopause

Diamond
Epidote
Garnet
Lapis Lazuli
Lepidolite
Lithium
Moonstone
Ruby
Stilbite

Menstrual

Jet – problems associated with
Lapis Lazuli – for pain
Moonstone – problems associate with
Rose Quartz – for pain
Unakite – problems associated with

Metabolism

Cacoxenite – improves
Chrysocolla – balances
Copper – improves
Labradorite – to balance
Marcasite – improves
Rhodonite – general

Migraine (also see: Headaches)

Amber – relieves tension and pain
Amethyst – to relieve
Fluorite, Blue
Lapis Lazuli – to prevent
Nuummit – to relieve
Rose Quartz – to relieve

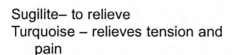

Sugilite– to relieve
Turquoise – relieves tension and
pain

Mood Swings

Lepidolite
Lithium
Stilbite

Motion Sickness

Sapphire

Multiple Sclerosis

Moonstone, Green

Muscular/Skeletal

Amazonite – reduces spasm
Aventurine – strengthens tissue
Chrysocolla – strengthens, for
cramping
Dolomite – helps to build, tone
Dioptase – cramping
Hematite – healing of breaks/frac-
tures
Iolite – relaxes muscles
Kunzite – treats disorders
Lepidolite – treatment of disor-
ders
Magnetite – relieves strain
Malachite – treatment of
breaks/tears
Morganite – strengthens tissue
Moonstone – muscle strengthen-
er
Selenite – treats deformities
Smithsonite – muscle relaxer
Stilbite – relaxes muscles

Tiger Iron – aligns spine, heals
breaks
Tourmaline – strengthens and
tones

Muscular Dystrophy

Ulexite

Nausea

Emerald
Jasper
Sapphire

Nerves/Nervousness

Watermelon Tourmaline

Nervous System

Amazonite – dissipates block-
ages
Amber – strengthens tissues
Aragonite – stimulates healing
Chalcopyrite – stimulates
Chrysoprase – system cell reju-
venation
Chrysocolla – general
Hedenbergite – heals at cellular
level
Hemimorphite – integration
Manganocalcite – heals at cellu-
lar level

Nutrition

Buddstone – absorption of
Fluorite – absorption of
Lazulite – absorption of

Old Age

- Buddstone
- Kyanite
- Rutilated Quartz
- Scapolite

Osteoporosis

- Amazonite
- Hedenbergite
- Howlite
- Malachite
- Scapolite
- Stilbite

Ovaries

- Amber
- Aventurine, Peach
- Carnelian
- Calcite, Golden
- Onyx, Black
- Topaz
- Vesuvianite

Pain

- Agate, Dendritic
- Amber – general pain relief, physical
- Amethyst – general
- Carnelian – removes blockage
- Clear Quartz – general
- Dioptase – pain of surgery
- Lapis Lazuli – pain relief, physical
- Magnetite – removes blockages
- Malachite – general
- Rose Quartz – pain relief
- Sodalite – general

Turquoise – pain relief

Pancreas

- Amber
- Bloodstone
- Blue Lace Agate – treatment of disorder
- Calcite, Green
- Carnelian
- Charoite – improves condition of
- Chrysocolla
- Citrine
- Garnet – treats liver and pancreas
- Jasper
- Malachite
- Moonstone
- Smoky Quartz
- Topaz

Panic Attacks

Lapis Lazuli

Parkinson's Disease

- Amethyst
- Cinnabar
- Opal
- Sugilite

Pineal Gland

- Amethyst
- Clear Quartz
- Opal
- Ruby
- Sugilite (Luvulite)

Pituitary Gland

Amethyst
Aquamarine
Chrysocolla
Garnet
Moonstone
Opal
Sugilite

PMS

Dioptase
Jasper, Green – reduces bloating
Magnesite – lessens symptoms
Moonstone – lessens symptoms

Pneumonia

Fluorite

Poisons

Amethyst
Bloodstone
Blue Lace Agate
Opal
Zircon

Postpartum Depression

Jasper – Bracciated, Red

Post Traumatic Stress Disorder

Pearl

Pregnancy

Amber – aids in childbirth
Danburite
Orbicular Sea Jasper
Lapis Lazuli – aids in childbirth
Moonstone

Prostate

Chrysoprase

Psoriasis

Blue Lace Agate
Conichalcite
Labradorite

Radiation

Amazonite – shields from
    microwave
Calcite, Blue – detoxifying
Clinozoisite – detoxifying
Herkimer Diamond – eases
    effects of
Kunzite, Yellow – eases effects of
Malachite – general
Sodalite – general

Recuperation

Peridot

Renal Disease

Jadeite
Nephrite

Reproductive Organs

Aventurine, Red
Carnelian
Eudialyte

Hedenbergite
Sulfur
Zoisite

Rheumatism

Agate
Amber
Azurite
Carnelian
Chrysocolla
Copper
Fluorite
Malachite

Sciatica

Malachite
Sapphire
Tourmaline

Scoliosis

Carnelian
Malachite

Seasonal Affective Disorder (S.A.D.)

Citrine
Citron
Sulfur

Seizures

Labradorite
Mesolite

Senility

Buddstone

Rutilated Quartz

Sexual Abuse

Zoisite

Shingles

Blue Lace Agate
Chrysoprase
Halite
Lapis Lazuli
Rose Quartz

Sinus

Aquamarine
Azurite
Blue Lace Agate
Larimar

Skin

Aventurine
Azurite/Malachite – skin problems
Conichalcite – skin problems
Dolomite – builds skin and nails
Gypsum – renew and enhance (elixir)
Hedenbergite – rejuvenation
Jade – soothe and smooth skin
Lazulite – skin problems
Moss Agate – topical treatment (elixir)
Rose Quartz – general
Scapolite – skin problems and rejuvenation
Spinel, Red – skin problems
Sulfur – skin problems
Zircon – general
Zoisite – skin problems

Sleep

Amethyst – calms/prepares for sleep
Celestite – sleep apnea, sleep enhancer
Cinnabar – sleep apnea
Lapis Lazuli – sleep apnea, peaceful sleep
Lepidolite – calms/prepares for sleep
Vesuvianite – calm/prepares for sleep

Smoking

Labradorite – assists with addictions
Staurolite – incentive and support to quit

Spleen

Azurite
Citrine
Fluorite
Peridot
Scapolite
Sodalite
Wulfenite

Stings, Bites

Moonstone

Stomach

Amethyst – treatment of disorders
Fire Agate
Fluorite, Green – disorders of intestinal track
Garnet – general
Jet – stomach pains
Labradorite – aids in digestion, regulation
Lepidolite – aids in digestion
Moonstone – digestive & elimination disorders
Sunstone – reduces ulcers & stomach tension

Stuttering

Blue Apatite – reduces

Taste

Topaz – improves
Tourmaline – improves

Teeth

Aquamarine
Dolomite
Fluorite
Howlite – calcium deficiency
Rutilated Quartz
Thulite – calcium deficiency

Terminally Ill

Eudialyte

Throat

Amber – treatment of disease
Angelite – inflammations/afflictions
Angelwing Anhydrite – throat disorders
Covellite – throat and mouth
Fluorite, Blue – general

Fluorite, Green – sore throats
Goldstone, Blue – general
Kunzite – general
Lapis Lazuli – sore throats
Morganite – strengthens
Nuummit – general
Rhodonite – strep throat infection
Stilbite – laryngitis
Sunstone – chronic sore throat
Tourmaline, Blue (Indicolite) –
    general

Thyroid

Aquamarine
Azurite
Celestite
Citrine – balances thyroid
Clear Quartz – to stimulate
Epidote
Galena
Garnet
Hematite
Kyanite
Larimar
Peridot
Rhodochrosite – to balance
Sodalite – to slow down
Vanadinite
Vesuvianite

Tissue

Carnelian – regenerator
Citrine – regenerator
Danburite – regenerator
Fire Agate – regenerator
Kunzite – regenerator
Peridot – regenerator
Rutilated Quartz – regenerator
Topaz – regenerator

Tonsillitis

Amber – to relieve
Blue Lace Agate – to relieve
Sodalite – to prevent
Tourmaline – to relieve

Toothache

Amber
Aquamarine
Jet
Lapis Lazuli
Malachite

Toxins

Amber – draws out
Bloodstone – draws out
Danburite – detoxifies
Dioptase – draws out
Emerald – flushes out
Fluorite, Yellow – draws out
Larimar – draws out
Lodestone – draws out
Malachite – draws out
Pearl – draws out
Serpentine – draws out
Wulfenite – draws out

Travel Sickness

Aquamarine – sea travel
Jasper

Trauma

Amber
Calcite, Blue
Hematite
Peridot

Tumors

Amethyst
Bloodstone
Danburite – removing
Sapphire
Smoky Quartz
Zircon

Turrette's Syndrome

Cinnabar

Ulcers

Blue Lace Agate – skin, stomach
　　ulcers
Chrysocolla
Diopside – general
Emerald – stomach
Quartz w/chlorite – general
Ruby – mouth, skin, stomach
　　ulcers
Selenite – general
Zircon – mouth, skin, stomach
　　ulcers

Urinary

Amber – to relieve ailments
Blue Lace Agate – to prevent, to
　　soothe
Calcite, Red – to relieve
Carnelian – to prevent
Jasper – bladder
Ruby – to relieve

Venereal Disease

Zincite, Red
Zircon

Vertigo

Lapis Lazuli
Quartz, Clear
Sapphire

Vomiting

Emerald
Lapis Lazuli

Warts

Blue Lace Agate
Smoky Quartz

Weakness

Carnelian
Emerald
Hematite

Weight Loss/Hunger Suppression

Apatite, Blue – hunger suppres-
　　sion
Diamond
Scapolite
Serafinite
Tourmaline, Green
Zircon

Wounds

Blue Lace Agate
Ruby

NOTES:

NOTES:

Emotional Healing

Abuse

Iolite – surviving abuse
Kunzite
Lapis Lazuli
Obsidian
Peridot
Tourmaline

Acceptance

Amethyst
Apatite – general
Carnelian – general
Chrysocolla – general
Quartz, Clear
Rose Quartz – birth, death, reincarnation

Aggression, to cool

Amethyst
Bloodstone
Rose Quartz

Anger, to alleviate

Amethyst
Blue Lace Agate
Bloodstone
Garnet, Red
Howlite
Moonstone
Peridot
Rose Quartz
Serpentine

Anxiety

Amethyst
Aventurine, Green

Calcite, Green
Chrysoprase
Hemimorphite – anxiety in children
Howlite
Lapis Lazuli
Lepidolite
Lithium in Quartz
Manganocalcite
Smithsonite
Black Tourmaline

Attachment Issues

Diamond

Balance – Emotional Body

Chalcedony
Chrysocolla
Fluorite
Galena
Lepidolite
Rose Quartz

Belonging, Sense of

Danburite
Heliodor, Green

Bitterness, Alleviate

Amethyst

Blockages

Kunzite
Kyanite
Lazulite

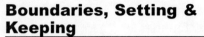

Boundaries, Setting & Keeping

Cavansite
Calcite, Honey
Copper
Smithsonite, Pink
Vanadinite
Zircon
Zincite

Brotherly Love

Tiger Eye, Blue
Tanzanite

Burnout

Amethyst

Calm, Increasing

Amethyst
Aquamarine
Aventurine, Peach
Calcite, Blue
Copper
Emerald
Garnet, Pink
Kunzite
Lapis Lazuli
Lazulite
Onyx
Rhodochrosite
Sapphire
Ulexite
Variscite
Wulfenite

Care of self

Rose Quartz
Kunzite, pink

Centering

Amber
Aquamarine
Chiastolite
Galena
Hematite
Moonstone
Zebra Stone

Chaos

Celestite
Cinnabar
Covellite
Galena
Gypsum
Pyrite
Selenite
Sphalerite
Sulfur

Choices

Chrysoprase

Cleansing

Blue Lace Agate – emotional

Comfort

Azurite/Malachite combination
Carnelian
Cavansite
Citrine

Danburite
Garnet, Pink
Malachite
Peridot
Rose Quartz
Sphene

Compassion

Bloodstone
Emerald
Hiddenite
Manganocalcite
Moss Agate
Pietersite
Rhodochrosite
Sugilite
Thulite

Composure

Amethyst
Aquamarine
Cerussite
Moonstone

Compulsive

Amethyst
Lapis Lazuli

Confidence, Self

Amblygonite
Cavansite
Chalcopyrite (Peacock Ore)
Citrine
Galena
Garnet
Hematite
Lapis Lazuli

Rhodonite
Rose Quartz
Ruby
Selenite
Tiger Eye, Red
Tiger Iron
Tourmaline
Variscite

Conflicts

Blue Lace Agate
Rose Quartz

Control, Releasing the Need for

Sugilite

Control, Self

Onyx
Rutilated Quartz
Zoisite

Consolation

Jasper
Sphene

Courage

Bloodstone
Ruby
Staurolite (Fairy Cross Stone)
Tourmaline

Crisis, In time of

Aquamarine
Clinozoisite

Epidote
Hematite
Staurolite

Criticism

Aragonite
Aventurine, Peach
Zincite, Yellow

Crying, to ease

Amethyst
Blue Lace Agate
Rose Quartz

Dark, fear of

Moonstone
Topaz

Decision making

Azurite
Rutilated Quartz

Delusions

Carnelian

Denial

Fluorite
Scheelite
Staurolite

Depression

Amber
Amethyst – general
Aragonite – genera

Botswana Agate, Pink
Celestite
Citron – reduces
Dioptase – reduces
Kunzite, Pink/Lavender/Orchid
Kyanite, Green – reduces
Lapis Lazuli – reduces
Lepidolite
Lithium – bipolar, manic depres-
　　sion
Petalite – general
Septurian Nodule – general
Smoky Quartz
Uvite – reduces

Despair

Calcite, Pink
Heliodor
Lapis Lazuli
Rose Quartz

Dignity

Garnet
Rhodonite
Spectrolite
Tiger Eye, Blue

Divine Love

Calcite, Pink
Kunzite, Pink

Doubt

Cerussite
Epidote

Ego, Surrender

Amethyst

Emotional Balancing

Chrysocolla
Galena
Green Millennium Stone
Kunzite, Pink
Lepidolite
Lithium
Moonstone
Pearl
Quartz, Clear
Rhodonite
Rose Quartz
Sodalite

Emotional Blocks

Kunzite
Kyanite
Malachite
Rose Quartz

Emotional Healing

Jade
Moonstone
Peridot
Quartz, Clear
Rose Quartz
Unakite

Emotional Pain

Calcite, Blue
Crazy Lace Agate
Clinozoisite

Emotional Protection

Zircon

Emotional Release

Morganite
Rose Quartz
Kunzite, Pink

Emotional Stabilizing

Quartz, Clear
Ruby
Tourmaline

Emotional Stress/Tension Release

Aventurine, Green
Calcite, Blue
Kunzite, Pink
Peridot
Quartz, Clear

Empathy

Turquoise

Enjoyment

Citrine

Enthusiasm

Rosasite

Fear

Angelite
Chrysocolla – reduces

Epidote – of losing hold on reality
Green Millennium Stone
Nephrite – reduces
Obsidian
Orange Millennium Stone
Topaz – reduces
Tourmaline, Black

Feelings, Hurt

Peridot
Rose Quartz

Feelings, Inner Worth

Labradorite

Forgiveness

Celestite
Morganite
Nephrite
Rhodochrosite
Rose Quartz
Selenite
Topaz, Golden
Zincite, Green

Friendship

Crystal Cluster
Diamond
Halite
Quartz, Clear
Rhodonite
Smithsonite
Turquoise
Zircon

Frustration

Blue Lace Agate
Pyrite
Rose Quartz
Stilbite

Gentleness

Anglesite
Bloodstone
Chrysocolla
Kunzite
Psilomelane
Rose Quartz
Sphalerite

Goals

Covellite
Heliodor, Golden

Gratitude

Chrysocolla
Eudialyte
Strawberry Quartz

Grief

Actinolite
Amethyst
Chalcedony, Blue/Purple
Emerald
Eudialyte
Hedenbergite
Jade
Lapis Lazuli
Obsidian
Peridot
Quantum Quattro Silica

Rose Quartz
Tourmaline
Tremolite

Guilt

Chrysocolla
Emerald
Rose Quartz
Sulfur

Happiness

Carnelian
Chrysoprase
Citrine
Fairy Cross Stone
Moonstone
Pyrite
Rose Quartz
Ruby
Rutilated Quartz
Sapphire
Sardonyx
Sunstone
Tourmaline

Harmony

Amethyst
Aquamarine
Bronzite
Dumortierite
Jade
Moonstone
Quartz,Clear
Rhodonite
Selenite
Sunstone
Tourmaline, Black
Tourmaline, Watermelon

Zoisite

Honesty

Blue Lace Agate
Celestite
Chrysocolla
Chrysoprase
Citrine
Emerald
Fluorite
Garnet
Heliodor
Scheelite
Selenite
Tiger Eye, Blue

Hope

Blue Lace Agate
Calcite, Pink
Chrysocolla
Chrysoprase
Citrine
Lapis Lazuli
Malachite
Moonstone
Sapphire

Humanitarian Love

Moonstone

Inferiority

Tiger Iron

Inspire

Emerald

Inspiration

Aquamarine
Citrine
Howlite
Petalite
Sphalerocobaltite

Jealousy, Alleviate

Peridot
Rose Quartz
Ruby included in Zoisite
Zoisite

Joy

Amazonite – promotes
Calcite, Green – promotes
Chrysocolla
Citrine
Dioptase – promotes
Eudialyte – promotes
Quartz, Clear
Rose Quartz
Ruby in Zoisite
Snakeskin Agate – spread to others
Sugilite
Topaz, Golden
Zircon

Judgment, of Self and Others

Chalcopyrite
Eudialyte
Leopardskin Jasper
Pietersite

Kindness

Azurite
Celestite
Chalcedony
Chrysocolla
Dolomite
Emerald
Kunzite
Rhodochrosite
Rhodonite
Rose Quartz
Sugilite
Tourmaline
Turquoise

Loneliness

Rose Quartz

Love, Unconditional

Chrysocolla
Kunzite, Pink
Morganite
Rose Quartz

Melancholy

Lapis Lazuli
Tourmaline

Motivation

Morganite
Rutilated Quartz
Tiger Eye, Red
Unakite

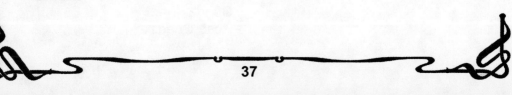

Negativity

Amber – removes negativity
Amethyst – removes negative thoughts
Rose Quartz – removes negativity
Ruby – removes negative thoughts

Nervousness

Aquamarine

Nightmares

Amethyst
Chalcedony
Hematite
Jasper
Ruby
Septurian Nodule
Smoky Quartz
Topaz
Turquoise

Nurture

Manganocalcite
Moonstone
Rose Quartz
Thulite

Overwhelmed

Amblygonite
Amethyst
Diopside
Zircon

Panic Attacks

Lapis Lazuli

Passion

Botswana Agate
Rhodonite
Ruby
Rubellite
Spessartine
Thulite

Patience

Amber
Azurite
Chrysocolla
Danburite
Strawberry Quartz

Peace

Apatite, Blue – general
Aquamarine – general
Blue Lace Agate – general
Celestite – general
Chrysocolla – general
Danburite – peace of mind
Indicolite – general
Petalite – general
Snakeskin Agate – inner peace
Sugilite – inner peace
Tourmaline, Watermelon – general

Perseverance

Lapis Lazuli
Quartz, Clear
Rose Quartz

Phobias

Aquamarine

Positivity

Aventurine, Green
Chrysoprase
Moonstone
Pyrite
Rose Quartz
Selenite
Sugilite

Prejudice

Sugilite
Wavellite

Purifying Emotional Body

Aventurine, Green
Jade

Rage

Amethyst
Aventurine, Green
Calcite, Green
Carnelian
Jade
Lepidolite
Peridot
Rose Quartz
Sugilite

Sedative

Blue Lace Agate – for nerves
Calcite, Blue – after emotional
    trauma

Self Confidence, Lack of

Azurite
Cavansite
Chrysoprase – aids in confidence
Hemimorphite
Tourmaline, Green
Zincite, Green

Self Esteem

Amazonite
Carnelian
Cavansite
Chalcedony – clears self doubts
Citrine
Copper
Hematite
Hemimorphite
Kunzite
Lapis Lazuli
Rhodochrosite
Rhodonite
Rose Quartz
Ruby
Sodalite
Tigers Eye – recognition of self
Zincite, Green

Shyness

Rubellite in Lepidolite

Stress

Amber – relieves
Amblygonite
Amethyst
Andaluscite – relief from
Chrysocolla – releases
Danburite – releases

Dioptase – relieves and releases
Dolomite
Epidote
Fluorite, Rainbow – repels
Lapis Lazuli – relieves
Mahogany Obsidian – relieves
Manganocalcite
Rutile, Red
Selenite – relieves

Trauma

Aqua Aura
Quantum Quattro Silica
Rose Quartz

Trust

Chrysocolla
Strawberry Quartz
Sugilite
Zoisite

Worries, Decreases

Calcite, Green
Chalcopyrite

NOTES:

NOTES

NOTES:

Higher Self

Affirmation Statements

Datolite
Quartz, Clear

Alignment

Sphene

Allowance

Garnet, Grossular

Altruism

Amber
Euclase
Golden Beryl (Heliodor)

Amplifier

Angelite – visualizations
Botswana Agate, Pink
Rhodochrosite
Quartz, Clear – healing, prayers,
  wishes

Ancient Wisdom

Amber
Herkimer Diamond
Moonstone
Record Keeper Crystal
Serpentine

Angelic

Angelite – communications
Aquamarine – contacting
Celestite – contacting
Danburite – contacting

Girasol
Morganite – contacting

Appreciation

Amethyst – general
Blue Lace Agate – of nature
Carnelian – general
Diopside – of women
Lapis Lazuli – general
Silver – nature and life in general
Zircon – general

Archangels

Botswana Agate
Herkimer Diamond

Artistic

Ametrine – growth
Botswana Agate – expression
Howlite – expression

Astral Travel

Calcite, White
Kyanite, Blue
Snowflake Obsidian

Attract Angels

Angelite
Blue Lace Agate
Celestite
Herkimer Diamond
Quartz, Clear

Aura

Actinolite – cleanses

Ametrine – disperses negative energies
Apophyllite – cleanses
Celestite – protection
Cerussite – cleanser
Chrysoprase – cleanser
Danburite – opens
Dioptase – cleanser
Dumortierite – opens
Fluorite – cleanses
Heliodor – cleanser
Herkimer Diamond – opens
Howlite – cleanses
Iolite – opens
Jade – cleanser
Kyanite – cleanses
Labradorite – to protect & stabilize
Moonstone– to balance
Rhodochrosite – cleanses
Rutilated Quartz – to clear, protect and balance
Selenite – opens
Sunstone – cleanser
Tiger Eye, Blue – opens
Tourmaline – cleanser
Zircon – to clear & strengthen

Awareness

Aquamarine – increases
Bloodstone – increases
Calcite, Honey – increases
Lepidolite – cosmic awareness
Moonstone – increases
Serafinite – increases

Awakening

Quartz, Clear

Balance

Ametrine
Carnelian
Chiastolite (Andaluscite)
Copper
Dolomite – creating balance
Fire Agate
Lapis Lazuli – etheric
Double Terminated Quartz – spiritual
Snowflake Obsidian
Tiger Eye – male/female
Zebra Stone

Blessings

Chalcedony, Blue/Purple
Larimar

Buddha

Bloodstone
Diamond

Celestial

Botswana Agate
Diamontina Quartz – interaction
Marcasite

Clairaudience

Angelite
Apatite
Cacoxenite in Amethyst
Celestite
Phantom Quartz
Snowflake Obsidian

Clairvoyance

Amazonite
Apatite, Blue
Azurite
Emerald
Herkimer Diamond
Pearl
Rutilated Quartz
Smithsonite
Topaz
Zoisite

Clarity

Amazonite
Apache Tear
Apatite,Blue
Apophyllite
Celestite
Chalcedony, Blue/Purple
Charoite
Copper
Emerald
Epidote
Fire Agate
Hemimorphite
Herkimer Diamond
Hiddenite
Lithium
Thulite
Tiger Eye, Blue or Cherry (Red)
Turquoise

Cleansing

Actinolite – auric
Amber – etheric
Calcite, Clear – etheric
Fire Agate – etheric
Howlite – auric

Larimar – etheric
Lazulite – etheric
Malachite – etheric
Tourmaline, Black – etheric
Uvarovite – etheric

Cognition

Lepidochrosite

Communication

Angelite – with spirits
Andaluscite (Fairy Stone) – with
   animals
Celestite – with celestial planes &
   guides
Labradorite – with higher forces
   or higher self
Lapis Lazuli – with spirit
Moss Agate – with plants
Pyrite – with consciousness
Rutilated Quartz– with spirit
   guardians
Sphene – with plants
Topaz, Clear– with nature spirits

Consciousness

Amethyst – shift
Azurite – increase
Celestite – higher planes
Labradorite – shift
Quartz, Clear – increase
Selenite – shift

Creativity

Amethyst
Charoite
Citrine

Covellite
Datolite – accessing the subconscious
Eudialyte
Kyanite, Black
Peridot – stimulates
Phenacite
Spectrolite
Spessartine – stimulates
Tibetan Quartz

Discernment

Iolite
Manganocalcite

Divine Love

Calcite, Pink
Kunzite, Pink
Rose Quartz

Divine Will

Onyx, Black

Dreaming

Amethyst – inspires
Cacoxenite in Amethyst
Jade – spiritual learning
Moonstone – enhances
Nephrite – spiritual learning
Onyx – enhances

Earth/Cosmos Connection

Diamontina Quartz

Ego, Surrender

Amethyst

Empathic

Iolite
Midnight Blue Goldstone
Zircon

Empowerment

Buddstone

Energy

Amethyst – transmits, stores
Axinite – increases sensitivity to
Buddstone – maximizes flow
Citrine – maximizes flow
Datolite – for energy workers
Diamontina – transmits
Goldstone – deflects unwanted energy
Hematite, Rainbow
Howlite – maximizes flow
Lingam – stores, absorbs
Malachite – absorbs
Moonstone – energy workers
Mesolite – energy workers
Petalite – increases sensitivity
Quartz – stores, transmits, maximizes flow
Snowflake Obsidian – increases sensitivity

Entities

Anhydrite – locates "unwanted"
Eudialyte – releases
Jet – releases

Etheric Body

Amber – purifies
Azurite – strengthens
Galena – balancing
Halite, Pink – purifies
Phenacite – stabilizer
Ruby – strengthens
Ruby included in Zoisite – strengthens
Zoisite – strengthens

ET Contact

Gypsum
Meteorite
Tektite
Tourmaline, Black
Uvite

Gaia Consciousness

Indicolite (Blue Tourmaline)

Gandhi

Ajoite

Goddess Energies

Euclase
Heliodor
Onyx
Vesuvianite

Godhead

Morganite

Grounding

Apache Tear
Amber
Bloodstone
Fluorite
Hematite
Marcasite
Smoky Quartz
Ulexite
Zebra Stone

Grounding during Psychic work

Jade
Marcasite
Vesuvianite

Healing, Spiritual Self

Amegreen

Healers and Healing on All Levels

Amethyst
Apophyllite
Aquamarine
Boji Stones
Cacoxenite
Calcite
Fluorite
Larimar
Moss Agate
Moonstone
Rubellite with Lepidolite
Selenite
Serpentine
Turquoise

Higher Realms

Amethyst
Moonstone
Quartz, Clear
Selenite

Higher Self

Amethyst – link to
Aquamarine – interface with body
Aragonite
Azurite – link to
Cavansite
Cerussite – interface with body
Galena – link to
Quartz, Clear – interface with
    body
Selenite
Spectrolite
Staurolite (Fairy Cross Stone)
Stilbite, Peach
Tourmaline, Blue – link to

Humanity, Serving

Bloodstone
Celestite
Dolomite
Dumortierite
Tourmaline, Pink

Humility

Amethyst
Bloodstone
Chrysoprase
Dumortierite
Quartz, Clear
Tourmaline, Black

Inner Peace

Snakeskin Agate

Inner Self

Aquamarine
Quartz, Clear

Insight

Charoite
Rhodonite
Tiger Eye, Blue or Gold

Inspiration

Aquamarine
Citrine
Ruby
Sphalerocobaltite

Intention

Cavansite
Larimar
Topaz, Blue
Vanadinite

Intuitive Knowing

Amethyst
Apophyllite
Cacoxenite
Creedite
Danburite
Iolite
Lapis Lazuli
Selenite
Sodalite
Sugilite

Tiger Eye, Blue
Unakite

Karma

Amethyst
Emerald
Tremolite

Kundalini Energy

Amazonite
Aragonite, Rust
Buddstone
Eudialyte
Heliodor
Lingam

Light, White

Celestite
Citrine
Herkimer Diamond
Smoky Quartz
Tourmaline, Black
Tremolite

Love, Unconditional

Morganite
Kunzite, Pink

Manifestation

Cavansite
Citrine
Lingam
Vanadinite

Meditation

Blue Lace Agate
Amethyst – stills mind
Aventurine, Peach – centering, quieting
Azurite – improves visualization
Celestite
Covellite
Datolite – reception
Fluorite, Blue
Heulendite
Idocrase – centering, quieting
Kunzite, Pink – trauma relief
Kyanite, Black
Labradorite
Lapis Lazuli
Lithium – discarding old baggage
Onyx
Petrified Wood – past life recall
Rutile, Red
Sapphire
Selenite
Snowflake Obsidian
Stibnite
Sugilite
Tremolite – surrender mind to higher self
Vesuvianite

Mediumship

Brazilianite
Cacoxenite
Chalcedony, Blue/Purple

Mother Theresa

Ellensburg Blue Agate

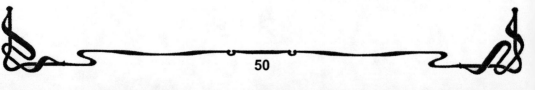

Nurturing

Manganocalcite

Past Life Recall

Amber
Apatite, Green
Carnelian
Diamontina Quartz
Dumortierite
Jade
Nephrite
Phantom Crystals
Serpentine
Tektite

Prayer

Angelite
Celestite
Chalcedony, Blue/Purple
Girasol
Larimar

Precognition

Celestite
Silicon

Protection

Apache Tear – psychic work
Aquamarine
Carnelian
Celestite
Chiastolite
Emerald
Euclase
Fire Agate – general
Fluorite, Blue
Goldstone, Purple – psychic work
Jade
Jet
Lapis Lazuli
Moonstone
Obsidian
Psilomelane
Snowflake Obsidian – psychic work
Staurolite (Fairy Cross Stone)
Tiger Iron
Tourmaline, Black – general
Zircon

Psychic

Angelite – opens to highest source
Buddstone – energizing
Cacoxenite – opens, stimulates
Celestite – opens to highest source
Citrine – opens
Herkimer Diamond – opens
Iolite – opening, grounding
Lapis Lazuli – opens
Obsidian – opens, stimulates, grounds
Selenite – opening
Septurian Nodule – psychic healing
Serpentine – opening
Sodalite – opens, stimulates
Sugilite – opens, stimulates

Reiki

Goldstone
Iolite

Reincarnation

Carnelian – to accept
Lapis Lazuli – to accept

Respect

Petrified Wood – ancient wisdom
Serpentine – general

Selflessness

Chrysoprase
Dolomite

Serenity

Amethyst
Carnelian
Chrysocolla
Diamontina Quartz
Emerald
Tourmaline, Black

Shamanic

Axinite – feminine energy
Celestite – cleanser
Danburite – Shamans Tool, protective
Datolite – feminine energy
Dumortierite – neutral energy
Quartz, Clear – healing
Tourmaline, All Types – masculine energy

Shielding

Obsidian

Spirit Guides

Blue Lace Agate – receptivity
Howlite – interaction
Jade – interaction
Nephrite – interaction
Orbicular Sea Jasper
Quartz, Clear – receptivity

Spiritual

Amethyst – spiritual upliftment
Brazilianite – messenger
Chalcedony, Blue/Purple – Integrity
Peridot – stimulates insight
Quartz, Clear – guidance
Lapis Lazuli – upliftment
Manganocalcite – unity
Rose Quartz – spiritual love
Sodalite – growth
Zircon – spiritual knowing

St. Francis

Ellensburg Blue Agate

St. Germane

Gem Silica

Tone/Toning

Aquamarine – meditation
Calcite – meditation
Goldstone, Blue – meditation
Manganocalcite – angelic
Sphalerite – meditation

Toxic Patterns/People

Zincite

Tranquility

Amethyst
Aragonite
Dioptase
Emerald
Rose Quartz

Transformation

Garnet
Hemimorphite
Lithium
Opal, White
Petalite
Sapphire
Snowflake Obsidian
Tantalite

Transition

Labradorite– personal empowerment
Lithium – personal empowerment
Stilbite, Peach – Life

Truth

Aquamarine – inner & universal
Celestite – spiritual, speech, thought
Charoite–Inner & universal
Danburite – spiritual
Iolite – Inner
Pietersite – universal
Sapphire, Blue – universal
Scheelite – speaking

Tiger Eye, Blue – universal

Unconditional Love

Pink Kunzite
Rose Quartz

Union, Sacred

Thulite

Unity

Garnet
Lingam
Manganocalcite
Quartz, Clear
Sea Jasper

Vibrations

Aqua Aura – stops negative
Citron – attracts positive
Moldavite – enhances attunement to
Obsidian, Black – attracts positive
Tourmaline, Black – stops negative

Vibratory Rate, Raising

Actinolite
Aragonite, White
Kyanite
Spectrolite – link to higher self

Vision Quest/Seeing

Apatite, Blue – seeking
Blue Lace Agate – improves
Hiddenite – quest

Kyanite, Black – tool
Kyanite, Blue – creative
Moonstone – quest
Peridot – vision with ultimate truth

Visualization

Angelite
Celestite
Kyanite

Will

Carnelian – right use of will
Calcite, Orange – right use of will
Citrine – activates
Eudialyte – right use of will
Moonstone – higher conscious-
    ness
Obsidian, Golden Sheen – acti-
    vates
Strawberry Quartz – activates
Sunstone – right use of will
Unakite – activates

Yin/Yang

Lepidolite – Yin
Rhodochrosite – Yin
Rubellite – Yang
Smokey Quartz – Yang
Sphalerite – Yin

NOTES:

NOTES:

NOTES:

The Chakras

Root Chakra (Muladhara)

Effect: Calms, dissolves tension.
Scents to assist with the root chakra include: Patchouli, Frankincense, Myrrh, Sandalwood, Cedarwood, Benzoin and Vetiver.
Note: C
Element: Earth
Connection to: Birthplace, culture, foundations
Influenced: Blood, spine, nervous system, bladder, male reproductive organs, vagina, testes

This chakra affects the sense of smell. The body parts associated with the particular chakra include: the bones, teeth, nails, legs, arms, intestines, anus, prostate, blood and cell structure. If this chakra is in harmony, you will feel a profound connection to nature, trust in nature's laws and a deep understanding of its cyclical ebbs and flows. If this chakra is not in balance, you will find an inability to trust nature and a tendency to focus on material possessions. You will feel a need to satisfy your own desires and wishes.

Some stones that are helpful in this area would be: Bloodstone, Obsidian, Carnelian, Red Jasper, Smoky Quartz, Ruby in Zoisite and Watermelon Tourmaline.

Lower Abdomen or Sacral Chakra (Svadisthana)

Effects: Stimulates desire, rejuvenates
Scents to assist with the Sacral Chakra include: Ylang-Ylang, Jasmine, Neroli, Sandalwood, Orange, Geranium and Rose.
Note: D
Element: Water
Connection to: Creativity, Sexuality, Emotions and Intuition
Influenced: Skin, mammary glands, female reproductive organs, kidneys

This chakra affects the sense of taste. It is associated with the reproductive organs, kidneys, bladder, pelvic area, sperm and all liquids and fluids of the body. If this chakra is in balance and harmony you will feel considerate, open, and friendly – a kind person who has no trouble sharing emotions or feelings with others. You may feel happily connected to life. If this chakra is not in balance you will feel unsure and unstable in sexual and emotional matters. You will not (or perhaps cannot) express your feelings and will suppress your natural needs.

Sacral chakra stones that can assist are: Red Jasper, Orange Carnelian, Topaz, Orange Calcite, Wulfenite and Citrine.

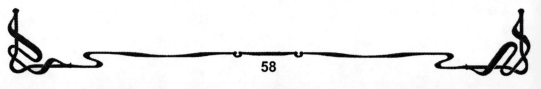

Solar Plexus (Manipuraka)

Effects: Eases aggression, pacifier

Scents to assist with the solar plexus include: Lemon, Juniper, Vertivert, Rosemary, Yarrow and Marjoram.

Note: E

Element: Fire

Connection to: Center of personal power, natural gifts, positive self ego

Influenced: Diaphragm (and the breath), adrenals, skin, digestive organs (stomach, duodenum, pancreas, gall bladder and liver)

This chakra affects sight. It is associated with the abdomen, lower back, stomach, spleen, liver, gall bladder and the autonomic nervous system. If this chakra is in balance, you will exude a feeling of wholeness, tolerance and acceptance of life and relationships. There is a natural balance of material and spiritual. If there is no harmony here, you won't trust in the natural flow and may feel a need to dominate. You will also have an emphasis on the material and a great need for material security.

Stones to assist in the Solar Plexus region include: Tigers Eye-Golden, Amber, Fuchsite, Citrine, Yellow Fluorite, Golden Beryl, Malachite and assorted Jaspers.

Heart Chakra (Anahatha)

Effects: Brings peace and understanding

Scents related to the Heart Chakra include: Rose, Rosewood, Bergamot and Jasmine.

Note: F#

Element: Air

Connection to: Center of compassion, healing, nurturing

Influenced: Heart, lungs, immune system (thymus and lymph glands)

This chakra affects the sense of touch and is associated with the Heart, upper back, rib cage, chest, skin, circulatory system, lower lungs and abdominal cavity. If this chakra is in harmony you will freely give of yourself. In combination with other chakras, it leads the way to understanding "Divine Love." You will feel more aware of the unity of all life. If not in harmony, you won't give love with sincerity, and may look for rewards instead of accepting love given by others.

Green Quartz, Aventurine, Dioptase, Green Tourmaline, Chrysocolla, Peridot, Variscite, Quantum Quattro Silica, Watermelon Tourmaline and Green Millennium Stone are just a few that can assist in the heart chakra area. Pink stones such as Rose Quartz, Kunzite, Morganite and Danburite can be used here as well.

Throat Chakra (Visshudha)

Effects: Brings harmony to speech and voice

Scents which are related to the throat chakra would include: Hyssop, Chamomile, Lemongrass and Sage.

Note: G#

Element: Ether

Connection to: Center of communications

Influenced: Throat, thyroid, nerves, eyes, muscles

This chakra affects sound and is associated with the lungs, vocal cords, bronchioles, throat, neck, jaw, thyroid, voice and nape of neck. If this chakra is in harmony, you'll know the balance of expression between silence and speech. You will be able to hear the inner voice and trust in your intuition. If this chakra is not in harmony, you'll have trouble expressing yourself despite much talking. You may be fearful of being judged and rejected, and afraid of silence.

Azurite, Angelite, Blue Lace Agate, Turquoise, Celestite, Chrysocolla, Aquamarine, Quantum Quattro Silica, Blue Topaz, Blue Tourmaline (Indicolite), Lapis Lazuli and Amethyst are helpful in working with the Throat Chakra.

Third Eye Chakra (Ajna)

Effect: Understanding and Harmony

Scents related to the Third Eye chakra would include: Rosemary, Lavender, Clary Sage, Peppermint, Frankincense and Spruce.

Note: High A (also OM sound)

Element: Electrical or telepathic energies

Connection to: Letting go of attachment, Divine relationship with spirit

Influenced: Pineal, Pituitary, Brain, Ears

This chakra affects all senses including the sixth sense. It is associated with the face, eyes, nose, sinus, cerebellum and pituitary gland. When this particular chakra is in balance you have an awareness of the spiritual side of being. You will invite intuition and inner awareness into everyday life and connect to the universe. If this chakra is not in balance, you will reject spiritual aspects and focus on the intellect and science. You only see the obvious, surface meanings and fear intuition.

For the third eye, it is suggested to use the following: Herkimer Diamond, Sodalite, Moldavite, Azurite, Indicolite, Lapis Lazuli, Kyanite, Labradorite, Lepidolite, Sapphire and Malachite with /Azurite.

Crown Chakra (Sahasrara)

Effects: Cosmic Aspects, Overcome self-limitations

Scents to assist in the area of the Crown Chakra would include: Frankincense, Myrrh, Benzoin, Sandalwood, Neroli and Lavender.

Note: High B or ee as in Bee sound

Element: Cosmic Energy

Connection to: Last layer of ego/attachment fall away

Influenced: Pituitary, Pineal, Nervous System, Brain

This chakra works beyond all senses and is associated with the brain, cerebellum and skull. If this chakra is in harmony, you are living with the knowledge of unity. You know that your self reflects the Divine and will abandon personal ego for Universal Ego. If this chakra is not in harmony, you will hold onto anxiety and fear and be unable to imagine cosmic Unity. You will live depressed and unsatisfied.

Some stones useful in this area would be: Moldavite, Quartz, Purple Fluorite, Labradorite, Sugilite, Lepidolite, Citrine, Golden Beryl (Heliodor), Amber and Amethyst.

Thymus Chakra (8th)

Effects: Connects us to our expression, confidence, and oratory

This chakra helps to strengthen your concentration and control over speech, allowing freedom of expression. This is also the chakra that assists in building the immune system.

Some crystals to assist in this area would include Aquamarine, Emerald and Malachite.

Heart Chakra (9th)

Effects: Love, kindness, consideration

Where the fourth chakra connects you to unconditional love, this ninth chakra connects you to the Universal Love. It helps you to remove all unwanted aggression and irritation. This energy assists in protecting you and giving you peace of mind.

Some crystals to use for this higher chakra would include Kunzite, Celestite, Apophyllite, Selenite, Kyanite, Morganite and Danburite.

Chakra Healing

NOTES:

Try these stones for your chakra healing:

- Cleansing lower chakras: Bloodstone
- Aligning chakras: Boji Stones or Yellow Kunzite
- Cleansing and Protecting ALL chakras: Tourmaline or Garnet
- Opening and Cleansing ALL chakras: Amber or Malachite
- Uniting Crown and Heart Chakras: Charoite
- Grounding Energy from Head to Toe (Crown to Base): Smoky Quartz
- Removing Blockages: Azurite, Bloodstone, and Lapis Lazuli

NOTES

As we are discovering, there are many, many more chakras then the traditional seven, which are referred to most frequently. A second heart chakra, between the heart and throat is opening in all of us. Study is constantly ongoing.

I listed the seven most recognized chakras here, as well as two additional ones, as impetus to get you started on your own research and recognition.

Crystal Information

Store Bound Rock Hound

First printed in 2003 at
http://www.themetaarts.com

I remember the first stone that was put in my hand six years ago. It was a moonstone – a pretty creamy colored, tumbled piece with shimmers when you turned it a certain way. I was fascinated. This spurred me on to learn as much as I could about "Mooney" the moonstone. I found several books that assisted me in this endeavor. Friends and acquaintances that had been into all things metaphysical and spiritual for many years longer than myself, recommended several other books. I read them all.

I would go to Cove Crystals, the local crystal shop and pick out more stones based on what I read in the books. Smoky Quartz for grounding, Snowflake Obsidian for balance and the list goes on and on. Before too long, I had a collection that any rock hound would be proud of! I felt a deep connection with some; others I was compelled **not** to hold and some were lukewarm or neutral. I worked with those I was drawn to and basically forgot the rest.

Later, I started helping out a couple of days a week at Cove Crystals and began to see a pattern emerge. If a customer utilized one of the many books in the shop, they would buy a lot of stones based on the list of properties in the book. Every page, I would hear someone exclaim, "Oh!! That is me for sure! I need that!" and off they would go to find it. Then there were those who would just walk around, maybe chatting about what problem they needed help with or what illness they wanted assistance with or how they wanted to keep negativity out of the workplace or their home. They would choose a stone for personal reasons only known to their selves. We would get out a book and read up on the properties and sure enough, it was exactly what they needed!

Linda, the owner suggested to me at the time that if I really wanted to assist a customer in the best possible way, to not be so quick to take out "the book" and just allow them to walk around, pick up and hold different pieces and to see what happened. Every time they used this method, the rock or crystal chosen was the perfect piece for the issue at hand.

How does this happen? What pulls a person towards a certain piece just because it may be sparkly, or a certain color? To hear an exclamation of, "Ohhhhhhhh, pretty!!!!!!" gives me pause to smile. Why?

This is intuition at its finest!

We all are naturally provided with this tool called Intuition. It can be invaluable when choosing stones or crystals to assist you with answers you seek or an issue you are currently experiencing. It is **the** best tool, in my opinion, to have at your disposal and it is totally free! Books are very helpful, but I have learned not to take the word of a book over my own intuition.

Why? Each person resonates at their own unique energy frequency and are naturally drawn to certain stones based on where they are at that particular moment in time. So, for instance, while one person may be strongly drawn to Kyanite, another may feel nothing. While both customers may want to use Kyanite to assist in meditation, reaching their highest guides, working on throat chakra issues, etc., it may not resonate for both. I truly believe that tuning in and really listening to your intuition assists you in making the absolute correct choice for you at that time in your life.

I am in such a unique position since my passion lies in helping others choose stones through the online community. I get to share my intuition with them, and they with me. We always choose just the right stone or crystal. It somehow amazes and humbles me every time!

Here are a few guidelines I use in everyday practice when assisting a customer with choosing the right stones for them. I also share these with those who are new to crystals, stones and rocks:

1) **Seller:** Take time and really listen to what the buyer has to say. Everyone has a story to tell and the story gives important clues as to what they really need.
   Buyer: Take time to listen to the inner self, your intuition. Never discount what you feel or hear.

2) **Seller**: I have never told a customer that a particular stone they have chosen is "wrong". I sometimes gently suggest others that may work well with the stone they have chosen, but will never second-guess the customer. Remember, we all work on very personal energy frequencies.
   Buyer: Don't get talked into anything that you truly do not resonate with. It is important to remember that you know better than anyone else what you need.

3) A simple rule of thumb is to remember the chakras and their corresponding colors. It's simple, and requires no big, heavy books to tote around. Go with a color that corresponds with the issue you are

currently working to resolve. Trying to get pregnant? Try some Carnelian (Red/Orange for the Root Chakra or Sacral Chakra) Dealing with some heavy emotional issues? Try Citrine (Yellow for the Solar Plexus) Communication issues? Try some Sodalite (Blue – Throat Chakra)

4) Your intuition will guide you to choose a stone, crystal or rock with the exact frequency you need so no matter which one you choose, it is your vibrational frequency and your intent that will work in concert with the stone, crystal or rock to achieve your goal.

So remember, books are great! They are extremely helpful and a wonderful resource. There are so many knowledgeable people out there who spend huge amounts of time to share what they know with us, through books, and I applaud and thank each one. Every author I have had the pleasure of reading, has made me a better person. I have learned so much! But remember, you possess the greatest tool of all – your intuition.

Take a breath, be still... what do you hear?

Copyright 2004 MoonCave Crystal

NOTES

Cleaning Crystals

As with all beginners, once I acquired my first crystals, I read everything I could get my hands on about them. Purchasing was, of course, just the first step in many, according to the books. Each book reminded me that cleaning the crystals was a necessary part of being their caretakers. And oh, how they all had different ideas and techniques to do so!! I was overwhelmed at the differences in opinions. Added to that, were the opinions of those I met who told me cleansing crystals had to be done a certain way. Talk about overload!!

I did find out, usually by trial and error, what worked for me and what didn't. One of my first purchased pieces was a lovely rainbow fluorite wand, which I immediately put on the dashboard altar of my recently purchased car. I loved that wand – it even color coordinated with the car with its deep rich blues, greens and purples.

A few days later, I noticed my fluorite friend had faded in color and intensity. I went back to the books. They did say sunlight was excellent for cleansing stones, so why was my fluorite fading? I was devastated.

Years later, my fluorite friend is still with me, faded and worn, but truly loved. He taught me a very important lesson – what you read doesn't necessarily hold true in all cases.

So this is what this article is all about. Just a few things I have picked up on my crystal journey to aid and share with you. Take and use what information you will, leave the rest. And remember, common sense is key. There is no "right" way or "wrong" way – just do what you feel in your heart is best for your crystals. My only rule of thumb is this, as I was reminded by a smoky citrine Elestial one day, if you would not do it yourself (i.e. lay in the sun for three days straight or be buried in sea salt), why would you do it to your crystal friends?

The Sun

Sunshine is wonderful for many crystals, Quartz especially love it. Putting your crystals out in the sun to cleanse is perfectly OK, just a few suggestions when you do so. Try not to put in hot, direct sunlight. Some crystals may fracture with sudden temperature changes or while under intense heat. Others will fade. Crystals such as Amethyst, Fluorite, Rose Quartz, Turquoise, Malachite, Tourmaline, some Lapis Lazuli and Quartz will react to direct sunlight.

Burying

Burying your crystals in the earth is again, personal taste. Since they come from the earth, it makes sense to bury them back there to cleanse and restore. Just a word of caution here, make sure you read up on this method using geological books, not metaphysical ones. A dear friend reminded me just the other day that if you're going to bury them in the ground, check the reaction of the local soil to the chemical makeup of your stones. Once below ground those lovely pyrites etc. can soon turn a spot poisonous. Remember, Arsenopyrite includes arsenic!

The Moon

This is my chosen and most recommended modality for cleansing any stone. The light of the moon will cleanse, without fading. It does not scratch or dissolve any stone or crystal. It is gentle and loving energy, much like a mother rocking a sleeping baby. Leave them out to soak up the energy and release any that is no longer needed.

Other Methods

In my experience, I have found one or two other methods that work quite well and are painless to all involved.

The first is a simple visualization technique. Just sit the crystal down on a table, altar, desk, etc. and visualize the stored energy you don't want slowly filling a balloon and flying away. Or visualize a mist moving out of the crystal into the universe to be transmuted into positive, love energy. What ever you are most comfortable with. It is all in the intent.

The second cleansing method I recommend is simply running under tepid (**not** hot and **not** cold) water for a few minutes and visualizing the unneeded energy flowing down the drain. Use pure water or spring water if you feel the chemicals in your water system would harm the crystal. I personally use Prill water for everything now, including running some over my crystals to clean them.

Last, but not least, do nothing. Crystals are energy and as energy, they cycle out those unneeded energies on their own, transmuting them to the positive love energy of the universe. If you have many, as I do, just know that the crystals help each other to purge that energy that is no longer useful to them.

Water

A customer shared a story with me recently. She lived by a lovely stream and read that putting her crystals in a mesh bag and allowing

them to soak in the stream was a wonderful way of cleansing them. Plus the added element of water would assist in reviving them. So, she put her calcite pieces in a mesh bag, placed them in the stream and when she went back the next day, the mesh bag was there, but her crystals weren't. It wasn't until a friend told her Calcite was water soluble that it dawned on her what had happened.

So, remember that some crystals are very sensitive and soluble in water. It is best not to soak such crystals as Halite, Selenite, Lapis Lazuli, Malachite, Rhodizite, Turquoise, Calcite and Celestite.

Sea Salt Bath

This was my favorite when I first began cleaning my crystals. Who wouldn't like a nice bath, right? Dry or mixed in water, this seemed the perfect way to cleanse many at a time. One day, I was cleaning some smoky citrine Elestials and, as I picked up a rather big crystal and began to move it towards the bath, I heard this: "I really do not like this! Would **you** want to be put in sea salt and left there?" I thought about it for a minute, first questioning my sanity at hearing voices, and then thinking twice about what I was doing. Think about it, would you want to be left in a salt bath for an extended period of time? My answer was, "No, I really

do not think I would like that." Since that day, none of my crystals have touched sea salt again.

A lot of crystals are easily scratched since their composition is made up of softer materials. Placing crystals in a dry sea salt bath will do just that – scratch them. Some of these crystals are Celestite, Calcite, Malachite, Rhodochrosite, Fluorite, Selenite, Moonstone, Sodalite, Turquoise, Hematite, Apatite and Lapis Lazuli. Of course, if these happen to be tumbled, the likelihood of scratching is minimized but still possible.

Separating Crystals, or Not

There is one thought shared with me quite often, and that is, that some crystals do not like being put with other crystals, or they may be detrimental if placed beside each other. I personally do not agree with this mode of thought, but as with all things, if it resonates with you, then it is your truth, and it will be honored.

Crystals are energy, just as we are energy. They each carry a specific vibration or energy signature. In my simple-minded way, I think of it like this:

Place fifty people in a room. They all have different and unique personalities, energies and dynamics. Some may clash, some may feel shy, some may be outgoing and some are so energetic they can lift the entire room. Crystals are much the same, energetically. However the difference is that they do not have ego or work at a five sensory level as most of us do. So when we state that one crystal should not be placed by another for fear of some unseen or unforeseen conse- quences, then we are truly stating that, from our five sensory perspec- tive, (our experience as a human being) that it must be true. Mainly because this is all we know.

I truly cannot think of one crystal that I would not place beside anoth- er. And in fact, the hundreds of per- sonal pieces I have and the hun- dreds of pieces I care take while they await new homes, have free reign of my space. None has ever been harmed.

Copyright 2004 MoonCave Crystals

NOTES:

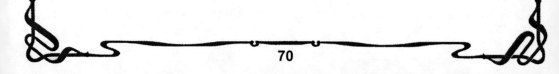

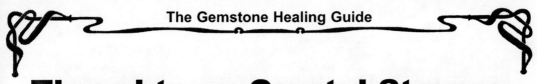

Thoughts on Crystal Storage

So, you have received a new batch of crystals from your favorite crystal shop. You have cleansed them using the method you most resonate with. You have programmed them to assist you in a particular (or general) purpose. Now, you ask, "Do they need to be stored?" "How do I store them?" "Are there any I should not put together when I store them?" All very good questions!! This article is dedicated to Terri who emailed me these very questions.

For me personally, none of my crystals are stored, as such. They are all laid on altars or tables or bookcases throughout my home. Even the ones that I take care of until they are sent to their new homes, are allowed to play with the others. However, there are cases when you want to keep those special, unique or rare pieces safe and sound. Or maybe you prefer to keep all of your crystals organized, labeled and away from each other so as to not cause any damage. So let's get started with the basics and tackle physical storage ideas first!

For those of you "rock hounds", who go out and collect your own specimens, or for anyone who has raw specimens in a collection, *The Complete Book of Rocks and Minerals* by Chris Pellant suggests the following: "House your rocks and minerals in trays within a drawer. You can easily make the trays at home to fit the drawer and the specimens, or you can buy them from specialist suppliers. Pack the more delicate items with tissue paper to prevent them from moving or rubbing against each other. Small, clear plastic boxes are also useful for storage."

At most variety stores, you can purchase a plastic chest with many small drawers in the hardware section for fewer than ten dollars ($10.00). These are wonderful to use as the drawers are small, to hold one specimen or a few tumbled pieces. They also allow you to label each little drawer with the name of the crystal. This is particularly helpful if you are just starting out. You may want to line the drawers with a cotton square or other soft material to keep the raw pieces from sliding around and causing possible damage. Another idea is to get some of poly "egg crate" material, also easily purchased in any variety store in the bedding section. They usually come in rolls so you can cut the amount you need to line a box or container quite easily. This works particularly well for keeping wands, points and larger specimens spaced safely away from each other.

Now for a thought on tumbled stones. Tumbled stones are, of course, prone to scratching and chipping, but they are, by far, much sturdier than their raw counterparts. Remember, softer pieces like Angelite and Calcite may scratch easier, so just use common sense if you choose to store these type of tumbled pieces. Many places sell sectional trays that would work just fine in the case of tumbled stones.

In *The Crystal Bible* by Judy Hall, she suggests the following for special care of your crystals, "When not in use, wrap your crystals in a silk or velvet scarf. This prevents scratching and protects the crystal against absorbing foreign emanations."

A few specimens need special attention that you should know about. Any crystal or specimen that should not be cleansed in water should also be kept in a dry, warm space. For instance, Halite is a type of salt crystal that will deteriorate if kept in a damp or humid location. Crystals such as Calcite, Celestite, Angelite, etc. also react in a less than positive way in damp conditions. For a listing of crystals in which water may be detrimental and/or other such elements, you can visit:
http://www.mooncavecrystals.com

Other specimens you should be particularly concerned about storing, are those that may contain arsenic or asbestos or other toxic materials in their raw form.

Realgar is a beautiful, bright red crystal that is amazing to look at. However, just be aware that Realgar also contains amounts of Arsenic, which may be absorbed through the skin. When working with Realgar, or other mineral specimens which may be toxic, just remember to wash your hands after use, do not put your hands to your eyes, face, mouth, etc. before washing them and keep these specimens in a small, plastic cabinet or specimen box, or wrapped in tissue paper and stored in a small box. Other minerals to consider packing in this way include: Cinnabar, Crocoite, Malachite and fibrous forms of Tremolite or Ulexite. A full listing of dangerous minerals and crystals that I, personally, know of can be found at the web site as well.

Also, keep in mind, that pieces that are tumbled or have been heat-treated have a reduced likelihood of absorbing through the skin and would be safer to use in healing, meditation and the like.

Elixir Warnings

The following are gems, stones or minerals that should **not** be used in elixirs.

Amazonite – use with caution, the color is a result of traces of copper (which is toxic)

Atacamite – poisonous (copper)

Auricalcite – poisonous (zinc and copper)

Azurite – poisonous (copper)

Boji-stones – unfit (contains some sulfur)

Bronchantite – unfit and poisonous (copper)

Chalcantite (AKA "blue shit") – poisonous (copper)

Chalcopyrite (peacock stone) – poisonous (copper and sulfur)

Cinnabar – poisonous (mercury/quicksilver)

Conichalcite – poisonous (copper)

Copper – poisonous

Chrysocolla (AKA Venus-stone) – poisonous (copper)

Cuprite – poisonous (copper)

Dioptase – poisonous (copper)

Gem Silica – poisonous (copper)

Galena/Galenite – poisonous (almost 90% lead)

Garnierite (AKA Genthite/ Falcondoite) – contains nickel

Halite – will dissolve in water

Hematite – will rust

Lapis Lazuli – poisonous (the pyrite inclusions specifically)

Magnetite – unfit (Iron, will rust)

Malachite – poisonous

Marcasite – poisonous (sulfur) (Marcasite has the same chemical make-up as pyrite)

Mohawkite – poisonous (copper, **arsenic**, etc.) (Keep away from children!)

Psilomelane – poisonous (barium)

Pyrite (AKA fool's gold; Inca-gold) – poisonous (Sulfur)

Quantum Quattro Silica – poisonous (Contains copper)

Realgar – poisonous (sulfur and **arsenic**) (Keep away from children!)

Stibnite (has Lead, Antimony)

Smithsonite (AKA Galmei, Zinc spar) – poisonous (zinc, may also contain copper)

Ulexite – unfit, as the rock will loose its luster when in contact with water; contains asbestos

Vanadinite – poisonous (lead)

Wulfenite – poisonous (lead and molybdenum)

General Rules

Avoid making elixirs and massage oils with any stone, mineral, or crystals containing any kind of metal (lead, copper, etc.).

If you don't know the chemical make-up of the kind of rock you have – avoid any blue or green stone, because most of the blue and green stones get their color from their copper content, especially the brightly-colored ones. Also avoid any shiny, metal-like stone, because most metals are toxic to humans.

And one last, general warning:

Stones containing arsenic (like Realgar) and mercury (like Cinnabar) should not even be worn nor handled without protective gloves etc. because of their extremely high toxicity.

Liz Gunther and Peggy Jentoft

NOTES:

References, Resources and Recommended Reading

The Illustrated Guide to Crystals
Judy Hall ISBN 0-8069-3627-4
Sterling Publishing Company, Inc
2000.

The Crystal Bible
Judy Hall ISBN 1-58297-240-0
Godsfield Press, Inc 2003.

The Book of Crystal Healing
Liz Simpson ISBN 0-8069-0417-8
Sterling Publishing Company
1997.

Crystalline Communion
Colleen Marquist & Jack Frasl
ISBN 0-9620201-3-3
Earthlight Inc. 1999.

Love is in the Earth
Melody ISBN 0-9628190-3-4
Earth Love Publishing House
1995.

Crystal Enlightenment
Katrina Raphaell ISBN 0-943358-
27-2
Aurora Press 1985.

Crystal Healing
Katrina Raphaell ISBN 0-
943358-30-2
Aurora Press 1987.

Quantum Quattro Silica, Orange
Millennium and Green
Millennium Information provid-
ed by:
Multistone, Intl. – Laurence
Hargrave, Owner
http://www.multistoneintl.com/index2.htm

Eighth and Ninth Chakra information supplied in part by:
Color Energy Corporation

Additional Notes

Additional Notes

Printed in the United States
110729LV00003B/184/A